MOTORCYCLES

Design   David West
                            Children's Book Design
Designer   Keith Newell
Editor   Yvonne Ibazebo
Picture Researcher   Emma Krikler
Illustrators   Simon Tegg and David Burroughs

First published in
the United States in 1992 by
Gloucester Press
95 Madison Avenue
New York, NY 10016

Library of Congress
Cataloging-in-Publication Data

de Vere, Charles
  Motorcycles / by Charles de Vere
    p.   cm. — (Let's look up)
  Includes index.
  Summary: A look at the technology of
motorcycles, from the earliest attempts at two-
wheel motorized transportation to today's
powerful machines.
  ISBN 0-531-17379-8
  1. Motorcycles—History—Juvenile literature.
[1. Motorcycles—History.] I. Title.
TL440.15.R63   1992
629.227'5'09—dc20   92-846   CIP   AC

Printed in Belgium

LET'S LOOK UP

MOTORCYCLES

CHARLES DE VERE

GLOUCESTER PRESS
New York · London · Toronto · Sydney

618431I

Contents

Modern bikes 6

Different designs 8

Suspension 10

Brakes 12

Four-stroke engines 14

Two-stroke engines 16

Gears and drive 18

Tires 20

Controls 22

Racing bikes 24

Special purpose 26

Engines 28

History 30

Glossary and index 32

About this book

You can decide for yourself how to read this book. You can simply read it straight through, or you can follow the arrows to find out more about a subject before you go on. The choice is yours!

Follow the arrows if you want to know more...

Introduction

Motorcycles are one of the most popular forms of transportation. Many people use them to get to work and back. Others use them to tour around the countryside. The very first motorcycles had small engines fitted onto ordinary bicycles. But today's machines are much larger and can travel at speeds of up to 185 miles an hour. Modern motorcycles also have bigger engines, better brakes and tougher tires.

Modern motorcycles can travel at speeds of over 185 miles an hour.

Modern bikes

Motorcycles are usually called motorbikes, and they are made up of many different parts. A motorbike has a metal frame which holds all the parts, including the engine and wheels, together. Fuel is fed in through the gas tank, and it is mixed with air in the carburetor before flowing into the engine. The main controls, such as the throttle and clutch, are on the handlebars.

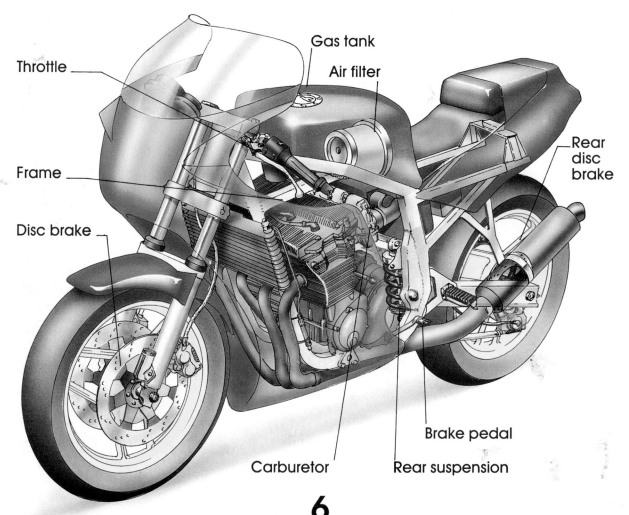

Throttle

Gas tank

Air filter

Frame

Rear disc brake

Disc brake

Brake pedal

Carburetor

Rear suspension

What is a fairing?

A fairing is a plastic molding that curves around the front of a motorcycle and the rider's legs. It makes the motorcycle more streamlined, so there is less wind resistance as it speeds along. Rear mirrors and turn signals may also be mounted on the fairing.

A motorcyclist in a race crouches behind the fairing.

If you want to know more about riding clothes, turn to History and development

PAGE 30

If you want to know more about motorcycle designs, turn to Special purpose

PAGE 26

How are motorcycles designed?

Modern bikes are designed on a computer screen. The system – called Computer Aided Design or CAD for short – is quicker and cheaper than building a new model for testing.

Different designs

There are various types of motorcycles, and each one has been designed for a different purpose. A very fast motorcycle has a large engine. The bigger the engine, the faster the motorcycle can go. Motorcycles that are used to travel around the streets have much smaller engines. Touring bikes have very large engines, and they are used to travel over longer distances.

A modern bike with a big engine.

Suspension

To help motorcyclists ride smoothly over bumps on the road, motorbikes have suspension systems, one at the front and one at the back. The front suspension is in the forks that hold the wheels together. It has springs that move up and down as the tires go over bumps. The suspension at the back is made up of a shock absorber and a spring. It is fitted to the motorcycle frame and wheel.

The suspension system helps motorcyclists ride over very uneven surfaces.

If you want to know more about how motorcycles move smoothly over the ground, turn to Tires

PAGE 20

How do the front forks of a motorcycle work?

The front forks have parts that slide up and down. The upper part of the tube contains air and the lower part is filled with oil, which acts as a shock absorber.

Air

Spring

Top fork

Swing arm

Plastic dirt protector

Swing arm moves up

Frame

Bottom fork

Suspension compressed

Hydraulic fluid

Linkages

Rear Suspension

Front Suspension

Brakes

Motorcycles need good brakes so that they can slow down or stop. Most modern bikes have disc brakes, at least on the front wheel. Older bikes have drum brakes. Disc brakes are fixed to the wheel and rotate with it. When the brakes are applied, a pair of pads press against the disc and stop the wheel from turning. The front brake is controlled by a lever on the handlebars.

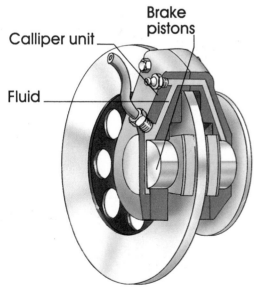

Calliper unit

Brake pistons

Fluid

Brake off: the disc spins in the gap between the brake pads.

Brake on: the pistons force the pads to squeeze the disc.

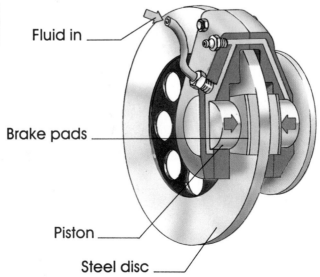

Fluid in

Brake pads

Piston

Steel disc

Why do modern bikes have holes in the disc brakes?

Disc brakes work by friction. But friction causes heat, and hot brakes do not work very well. As the disc brake warms up, the holes allow the heat to escape into the air passing over the disc. The brake in the picture has a piston on each side.

Hole

If you want to know how drum brakes work, turn to History and development **PAGE 30**

13

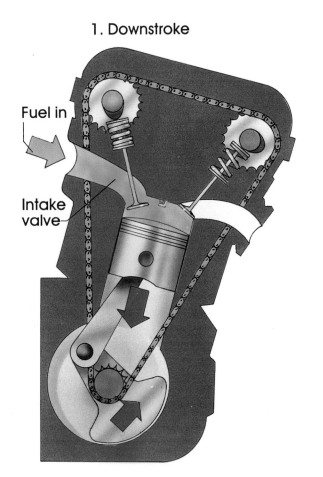

1. Downstroke

Fuel in

Intake valve

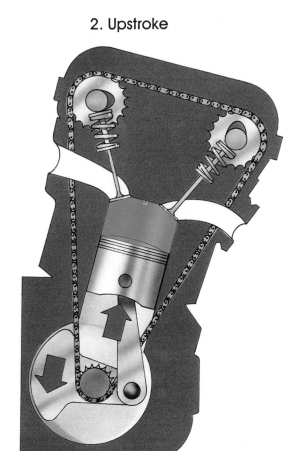

2. Upstroke

Four-stroke engines

Most bikes with engines of more than 250cc have four-stroke engines. On the first downstroke, gasoline and air are sucked into the engine through an intake valve. On the second stroke the piston rises and compresses the fuel. Then the spark plug explodes the fuel, forcing the piston down again. On the fourth stroke, the piston moves up and forces out the exhaust gases.

3. Explosion

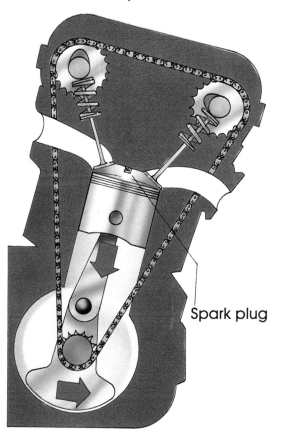

Spark plug

4. Upstroke

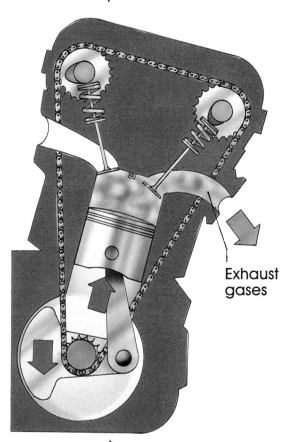

Exhaust gases

If you want to know more about other engines, turn to Two-stroke engines

PAGE 16

What is cc?

There are many different sizes of engines, and they are measured in cubic centimeters, or cc. This tells us how much space there is inside the engine.

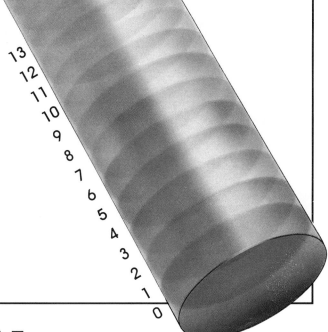

13 12 11 10 9 8 7 6 5 4 3 2 1 0

Two-stroke engines

Most early motorcycles and many of today's smaller machines use two-stroke engines. In a two-stroke, the piston moves up and down twice to produce power. To lubricate the engine, oil is mixed with the gasoline. Two-strokes are smaller and simpler than four-strokes, and so they are easier to care for. But they make more noise and use more fuel.

The diagrams (below) show how a two-stroke engine works. As the piston moves up (1), it compresses the fuel which is exploded by the spark plug (2). As the piston moves down (3), exhaust gases leave the engine (4). At the end of the downstroke (5), new fuel passes above the piston for the next upstroke (6).

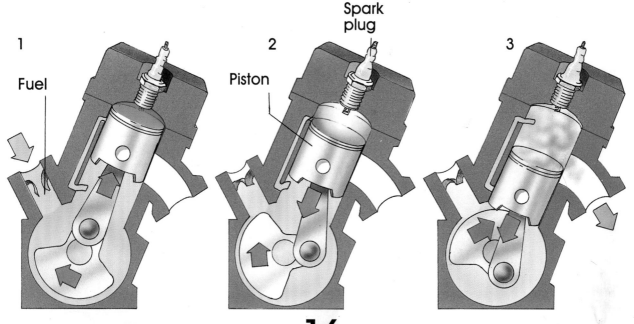

1

Fuel

2

Spark
plug

Piston

3

What type of fuel do motorcycles use?

Most motorcycles use gasoline as a fuel. In a four-stroke engine, gasoline is mixed with air in the carburetor before flowing into the engine. Oil is added to the gasoline in a two-stroke.

If you want to know how cylinders are arranged in engines, turn to Engines

PAGE 28

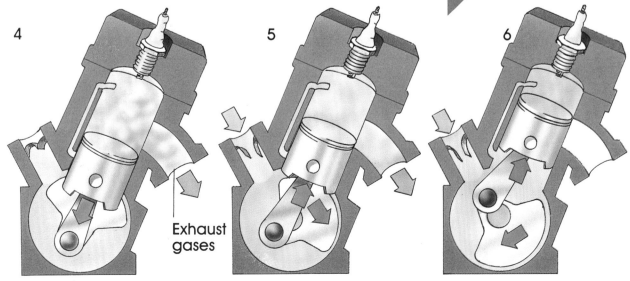

4

5

6

Exhaust gases

Gears and drive

Most motorcycles have gears that are used to make the bike go faster or slower. The power from the engine is sent to the rear wheel through the transmission system, which is made up of a clutch, gear box, and final drive. When shifting gears, the rider uses a clutch to disconnect the engine from the transmission. Then the power is carried by the final drive to the back wheel.

How many gears do bikes have?

Different types of motorcycles have different numbers of gears. Small bikes have up to three gears, and others may have up to six. The speedway bikes in the picture have one gear.

Do all bikes have a chain? PAGE 31

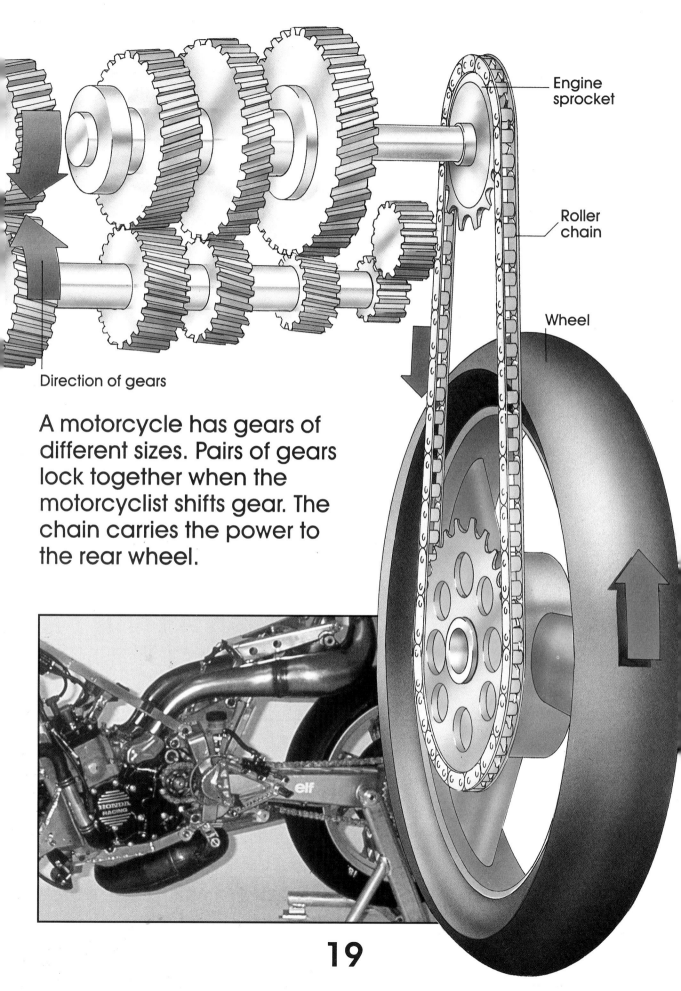

Engine
sprocket

Roller
chain

Wheel

Direction of gears

A motorcycle has gears of different sizes. Pairs of gears lock together when the motorcyclist shifts gear. The chain carries the power to the rear wheel.

elf

HONDA
RACING

19

Tires

Tires press against the ground and enable the bike to move along the road. The surface of a tire is called its tread, and different types of tread are used for different motorcycles. An off-road bike (below), used for scrambling, has knobbly tires that help it grip the road. Racing bikes have radial tires with treads or smooth tires called slicks.

Why use slicks and treads?

Slicks are smooth tires with no treads. On a dry, even surface - such as a race track - they provide a better grip than a tire with treads and allow the rider to turn corners faster. But slick tires cannot grip a wet surface. So if it rains, riders fit treaded tires (below left) to their machines.

Tread tires

Slick tires

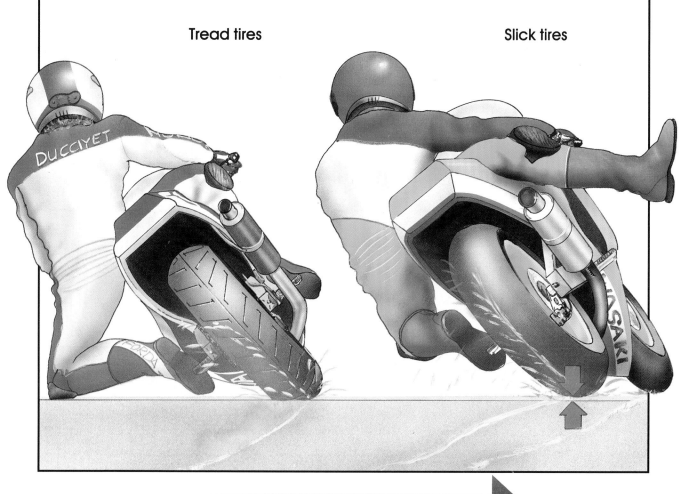

Find out more about tires in Special purpose → PAGE 26

Controls

A rider controls a motorcycle with his or her hands and feet. There are three controls on the handlebars. On the right side is the lever for the front brake and the twist-grip throttle for controlling engine speed. On the left is the clutch lever. The handlebars also steer the bike. The rider's left foot works the gear lever and the right foot controls the back brake.

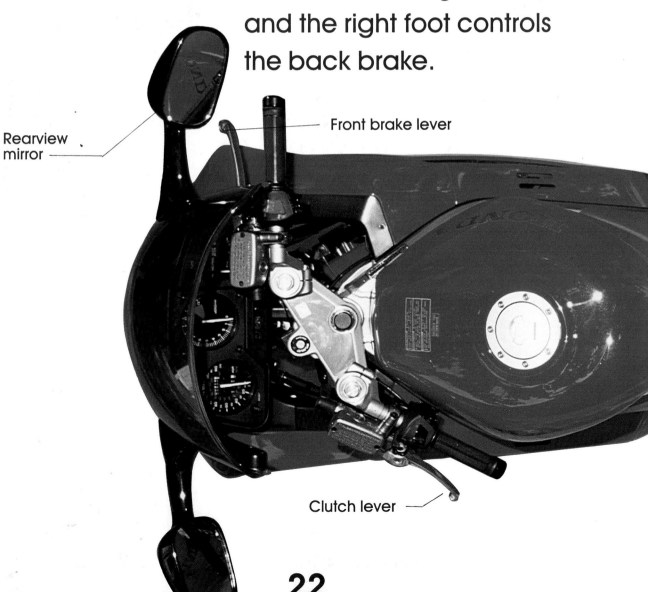

Front brake lever

Rearview
mirror

Clutch lever

If you want to find out about torque, turn to **Engines** ➡ PAGE 28

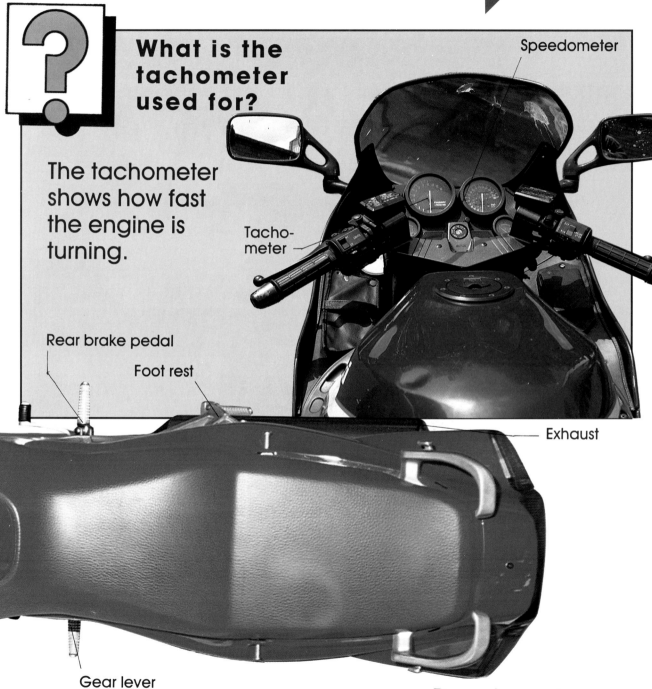

? What is the tachometer used for?

The tachometer shows how fast the engine is turning.

Speedometer

Tacho-meter

Rear brake pedal

Foot rest

Exhaust

Gear lever

The controls on a motorcycle are easy to reach.

Rearview mirrors help riders see the traffic coming up behind them.

23

Racing bikes

Motorcycle racing is one of the most popular motor sports. Large racing bikes travel around special circuits at speeds of over 185 miles an hour. The motorcycles race in classes, according to the size of the engine. They usually have a fairing to streamline the front. Some have fuel injection or a turbocharger for more power. There are also races for bikes with sidecars.

To find out about the fastest bikes, turn to Special purpose

PAGE 26

Why do passengers hang out of sidecars?

When a bike with a sidecar goes around a bend, the wheel of the sidecar tends to lift off the road. So passengers lean out and use their weight to stop this from happening.

A motorbike with a passenger hanging out of the sidecar.

Special purpose

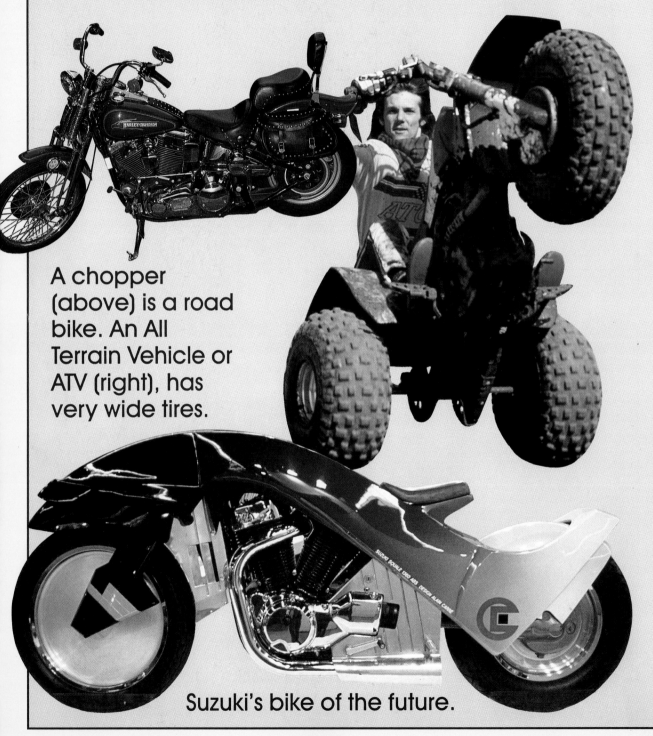

There are many different types of motorcycles that people use today.

A chopper (above) is a road bike. An All Terrain Vehicle or ATV (right), has very wide tires.

Suzuki's bike of the future.

Motorbikes used in cross country racing, are tough and light-weight.

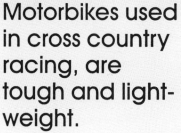

Ice racing bikes (left) have tires with metal spikes for traction.

The fastest bikes are dragsters (below), which cover one-quarter mile in 7 seconds.

Engines

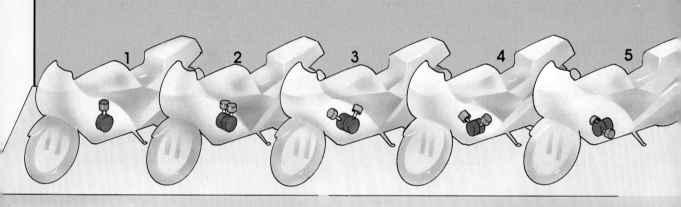

1   2   3   4   5

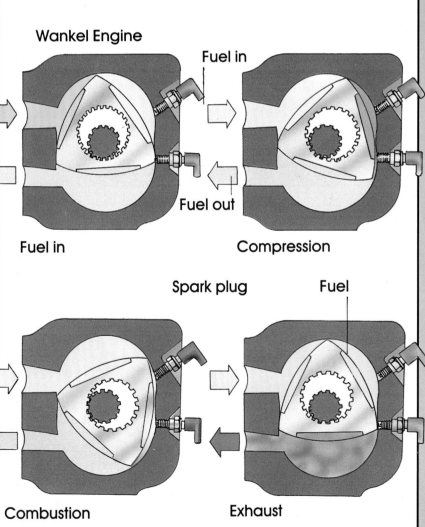

Wankel Engine

Fuel in

Fuel out

Fuel in

Compression

Spark plug

Fuel

Combustion

Exhaust

Engine layouts

1 Single cylinder
2 Twin
3 V-twin
4 V-twin, transverse
5 Flat twin
6 Triple cylinder
7 In-line four
8 V-four
9 Flat four
10 Flat four, in-line

The Wankel engine (left) has a cylinder, two spark plugs, and a triangular "cylinder."

Motorcycle engines have between one and four cylinders arranged in various ways. They may be mounted across the frame of the machine or in line with it (see diagram below). The largest four-cylinder engines are cooled by water.

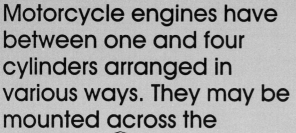

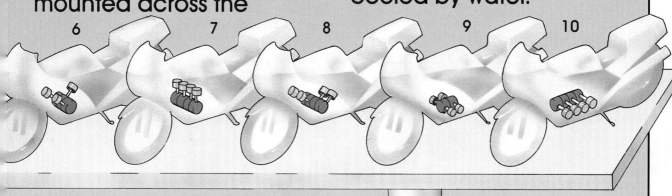

6   7   8   9   10

The strength of the turning force exerted by an engine is called torque. Maximum torque is produced at a particular engine speed. A rider keeps the engine near that speed when shifting gear.

History

Motorcycles have been around for over a 100 years, and there have been many improvements in engine designs.

A
French motor-assisted bicycle of 1869

B
A typical German Daimler bike

E
490 cc Norton 'International' of 1933

F
Velocette KTT of 1950 with a 348 cc engine

I
BSA 'Rocket' of 1970 with a 740 cc engine

J
Suzuki GS750 of 1977 with a 742 cc engine

Apart from chain drives, motorbikes may use a belt drive or a shaft drive (right).

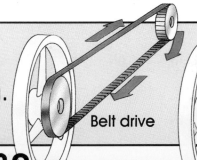

Belt drive

Shaft drive

Drum brake

On

Brake pads

Off

Brake cable

Brake shoe

Pad

Back wheels on many bikes have drum brakes (far left). Mopeds may have simple calliper brakes (left).

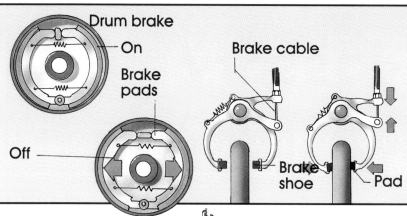

C

Indian of 1911 with a 998cc V-twin engine

D

998cc Brough-Superior of 1929

G

246cc Moto Guzzi "Albatros" of 1947

H

Harley-Davidson 998cc V-twin of 1945

K

Yamaha FZR 1000R of 1991 (1000 cc)

Riding gear has changed from outdoor clothes (1) to crash helmets (2) and full leathers (3).

Glossary

Carburetor A unit where gasoline and air are mixed before it flows into the engine.

Clutch A lever on the handlebar used to disconnect the engine from the transmission. It is used when a motorcyclist wants to shift gears.

Throttle This controls the amount of fuel going into the engine and the engine speed. It is operated by twisting a grip on the handlebar.

Turbocharger A pump that forces extra fuel into the engine to produce more power.

Index

brakes 5, 12-13, 22, 31

carburetor 6, 17, 32
clutch 6, 18, 22, 32
controls 6, 22-3

drive 18, 31

engines 5, 6, 8, 14-17, 25, 28-9

fairing 7, 24
fuel 6, 14, 16, 17

gears 18-19

racing bikes 5, 19, 20, 24-5, 27

sidecars 24, 25
speed 5, 27

suspension system 10-11

tachometer 23, 29
throttle 6, 22, 32
tires 5, 20-1
torque 29
transmission system 18
turbocharger 24, 32

PHOTOCREDITS
Pages 5, 7,20 and 24: Aladdin's Lamp; pages 6, 15, 19, 23 and 26 top left: Roger Vlitos; page 10: J. Allan Cash Photo Library; pages 11, 16, 22-23, 26 top right and bottom and 27 all: Frank Spooner Pictures; page 17: Nicholls.